Gardening WITH THE EXPERTS

ORCHIDS

PHILIP TOMLINSON

HARLAXTON
PUBLISHING

*Front cover: A **Dipodium** orchid.*
*Opposite title page: A **Vanda** hybrid.*

Photographs: Leo Meier courtesy Weldon Trannies: opposite title page, pages 6, 14, 24-25.
Philip Thomlinson: pages 7, 8, 9, 10, 11, 12, 13, 17, 18, 19, 20, 21, 22, 26, 27, 28, 29, 30,
32, 34, 35, 36, 37, 38, 40, 41, 42, 43, 44, 45, 46.
Weldon Trannies: front cover.

Published by Harlaxton Publishing Ltd
2 Avenue Road, Grantham, Lincolnshire, NG31 6TA, United Kingdom.
A Member of the Weldon International Group of Companies.

First published in 1990 (Limp)
Reprint 1991 (Cased)
Reprint 1992 (Cased)
Reprinted 1993

© Copyright Harlaxton Publishing Ltd
© Copyright design Harlaxton Publishing Ltd

Publishing Manager: Robin Burgess
Illustrations: Kathie Baxter Smith
Typeset in UK by Seller's, Grantham
Produced in Singapore by Imago

British Library Cataloguing-in-Publication data.
A catalogue record for this book is available from the British Library.
Title: Gardening with the Experts: Orchids.
ISBN:1 85837 025 6

Gardening WITH THE EXPERTS

ORCHIDS

CONTENTS

INTRODUCTION   7

WHAT IS AN ORCHID?   9

CULTIVATION   15

PESTS AND DISEASES   33

PLANT PROPAGATION   39

SOURCES OF PLANTS AND INFORMATION   43

INDEX   47

INTRODUCTION

Many gardeners appreciate the delicate and intricate beauty of orchid flowers but assume that orchids are either expensive or difficult to grow and require extensive growing facilities. As a result, few gardeners attempt to grow them.

However, if you can grow the usual garden flowers and vegetables, you will be equally successful with orchids. This book attempts to dispel the many commonly held fallacies about one of the greatest of all plant groups — orchids.

Sarcochilus hartmanii, *a quick-growing Australian native which produces large specimen plants and a spectacular display when well grown.*
*Page opposite: An **aranda** hybrid.*

WHAT IS AN ORCHID?

Orchids are one of the largest of all plant families. Most people have orchids growing in their gardens or close by but do not realise they are orchids because the flowers are insignificant. It is the large, brightly coloured flowers given on special occasions or seen in corsages that attract attention.

For reasons best known to themselves orchids have developed a remarkable diversity of plant variety and floral forms in particular, it is the greatest variation seen in any of the world's great plant families. This aspect makes these long-lived perennials exciting and desirable additions to any collection of cultivated plants.

Some of the plants are only millimetres tall, with dark, inconspicuous flowers. Such plants are of botanical interest only. The vast number of species orchids—those able to be found growing naturally in their countries of origin—and man-made hybrids will satisfy even the most fastidious grower. Variations in plant size and form, flower size, colour and season of flowering ensure varieties are available to fit every grower's need. Those commonly cultivated range in size from 150mm up to 1 metre tall, with flowers of every colour imaginable, except black. Flowers may be produced individually or in dense bunches, each ranging in size from just a few millimetres up to 300mm wide.

There are two different growth forms.

The MONOPODIAL —such as *vandas* or *phalaenopsis*, continue to grow upwards, the new year's growth being an extension of the previous year's growth.

The SYMPODIAL —such as *cattleyas* or *cymbidiums*, produce a new season's growth from the base of the previous year's.

This book shows some of the orchids available, especially those which novice growers will find easiest to cultivate.

The natural habitats of orchids extend from the tropics up to the Arctic and down

Pterostylis graminea *is one of many similar orchids that grow widely throughout Australia and New Zealand but are often overlooked.*
Page opposite: **Cymbidium** *Touchstone 'Mahogany', a very floriferous miniature producing pendulous spikes.*

Pleione formosana produces single flowers which are large for the size of the plant.

to the subantarctic islands, from sea-level up to the snowline on high mountains, and from hot, humid lowland forests to deserts. Accordingly, types can be found that suit all growing conditions.

Orchid flowers are distinguished from others because one of the petals has evolved into a distinctive and specialised structure known as the lip, a "landing pad" for pollinating insects. The other five main flower parts (three sepals and two petals) are more conventionally shaped. The separate reproductive parts of other flowers have become fused in orchids to produce the column. The pollen, which is in a cap rather than loose, is found at the apex of this structure, while the stigma surface lies below. It is a characteristic of most orchids that you can take a vertical line down through the column and lip, and one side

Dendrobium 'Ellen' is a quick-growing Australian hybrid producing many spikes, each with a large number of individual flowers.

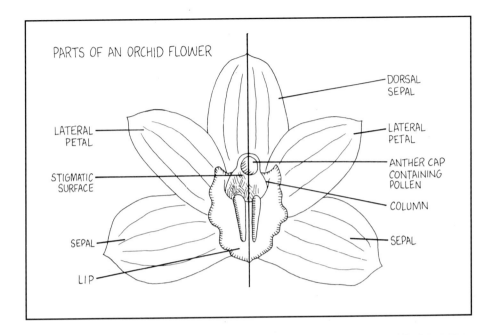

PARTS OF AN ORCHID FLOWER

DORSAL SEPAL

LATERAL PETAL

LATERAL PETAL

ANTHER CAP CONTAINING POLLEN

STIGMATIC SURFACE

COLUMN

SEPAL

SEPAL

LIP

will be a mirror image of the other.

Many orchid flowers are long-lived either as cut flowers or when left on the plant. Popular varieties often last four to six weeks in perfection; some last up to three months. Also, many emit a delightful fragrance. If you buy orchid flowers from florists, you will find that you will be able to grow many of these yourself. In fact, you can often purchase a whole plant for not much more than you pay for a single flower, and you will also get more flowers next year!

Most orchids characteristically produce pseudobulbs — much-thickened stems joined by a rhizome. These structures, each of which usually represents one year's growth, are important water conservation organs, especially necessary when plants come from potentially stressful habitats high in trees or in deserts. Pseudobulbs come in all shapes and sizes—metres tall in

Aërides 'Amy Ede' *exhibits the monopodial type of growth.*

Dendrobium 'arachnites' is a compact species which shows the swollen stems, or pseudobulbs, characteristic of many orchids.

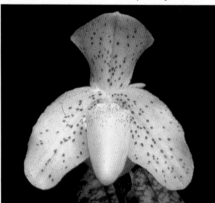

Paphiopedilum 'concolor' is a typical sympodial orchid.

some plants, absent in others. Most will produce flowers for only one year. After that they support the plant's continuing growth until they die between three to five years later.

The majority of commonly cultivated orchids grow naturally as *epiphytes* — that is, they are found growing on a host tree but do not extract nutrients from it as do parasites. A few grow on rocks or in thick pads of moss and leaf detritus on the forest floor. All those commonly grown adapt readily to container cultivation.

It is appropriate to consider typical growth cycles. Most go through a similar cycle of growth and development. In the spring new shoots appear, which quickly develop. In autumn the new pseudobulbs mature, and flowering will follow. Some plants will rest before flowering, others after flowering is completed. Most will rest during winter. It is important to observe a particular plant's resting requirements if maximum success is to be obtained. Some plants, like *cymbidiums*, *paphiopedilums* and *phalaenopsis* require a temperature drop for two to six weeks for successful bud initiation. *Cymbidiums*, can be grown in a glasshouse, on a porch or patio for most of the year according to your regional climate. During summer they must be put outside in partial shade, in a fresh, airy environment where cooler temperatures are experienced, otherwise flowering will not occur.

Sarcochilus ceciliae *is an Australian native which grows naturally on mossy rocks.*

Oncidium stramineum* x *aurisasinorum
can be grown on a branch to simulate the natural habitat of tree orchids.

CULTIVATION

For the growth of *any* plant, certain essential requirements must be met or it will die. These are:

- suitable temperature levels;
- an adequate supply of water;
- plenty of fresh, moving air;
- suitable light levels; and
- a suitable and adequate supply of essential mineral salts.

Successful cultivation provides all the above to the level required by each plant. If any one requirement is not met at the optimum level, full growth and flower production as allowed by the genetic make-up will not be achieved. All the following conditions described are involved with the provision of the above essentials.

TEMPERATURES

Because orchids display such wide natural diversity, growers often speak of cool, intermediate and warm growing types, representing the temperature requirements necessary for their cultivation. in *broad terms*, this information can assist in the selection of plants.

These average temperatures can be departed from once experience is gained with the plants concerned. Small plants require temperatures 5°C to 7°C higher. If cooler temperatures are experienced, growing plants somewhat dryer can assist.

GROWING FACILITIES

It is commonly believed extensive and expensive growing facilities are required for orchids. Depending on your regional

---

TEMPERATURE GROUPINGS
Minimum requirements — in degrees Celsius

Growing Type	Winter		Summer	
	Night	Day	Night	Day
Cool (C)*	10-15	7-10	15-18	ambient (7-15)
Intermediate (I)*	18-20	12-15	18-25	15-18
Warm (W)*	20-25	18-20	20-25	18-20

*Temperature requirements shown for plants illustrated in this book.

---

*Page opposite: An intergeneric hybrid, **Aranda (Arachnis** x **Vanda**).*

TRAY OF GRAVEL

orchid growers have one major failing—they like to talk about their hobby; you can therefore easily discuss with them what facilities are required for the main plant groupings suited to growing in your area.

If you grow plants indoors and some require additional heat, this can be most conveniently supplied by heat boards or propagating beds. Provided the root area is kept warm, heating the whole growing area is not required; quite often there is enough radiant heat for the remainder of the plant.

Inside most homes, the humidity is lower than most orchids appreciate. This can be increased by growing the plants on a tray of gravel with water kept to a level just below the surface of the gravel. Plants in pots standing on the gravel will benefit from the rising humidity.

In warmer regions, if you grow plants outside, an area below the outer branches of a tree will often be satisfactory. Place the pots on a small bench or bricks to allow free circulation of air, yet prevent insects entering the pots.

climate the majority will happily grow and thrive either in the home, under glasshouse conditions, or in those available in almost all gardens in warm regions.

Go to any orchid show and talk to the exhibitors. You will find some of the best plants have been grown at home, in the lounge, kitchen or bathroom, greenhouse conservatory or warm window-sill. It is all about choosing the right type of plant for the particular conditions and facilities available. Because some orchid flowers look delicate, it does not necessarily follow that the plants are delicate. In fact, most orchids are remarkably tough — I once divided a large *cymbidium* with an axe, to have all the plants obtained break into copious bloom the following year. While the required conditions vary between types, in general terms if conditions are comfortable for you, the grower, then the orchids will be comfortable too. If you want to find out what orchids can be easily grown in your area, go to one of the many orchid shows run by societies throughout the country. You will find that most serious

GROWING MEDIA
Orchids can be grown in clay or plastic pots, although provision of extra drainage holes are advantageous. Orchid roots need a constant supply of moisture but must also receive fresh air if they are to survive.

Orchids have been grown in many and varied media, ranging from osmunda fibre, rice husks, wood bark and even gravel. The final choice depends on cost, suitability and availability, but these days the use of chopped pine bark usually meets most requirements. It is readily available and comparatively inexpensive. Generally, bark pieces should range in size from 3-12mm, with all dust removed. Various additives can be included, such as scoria, pumice or

CYMBIDIUMS

These popular, colourful, easily grown varieties are especially suitable for cool conditions. They range from the larger standard types—cool growing—to the miniatures, many of which prefer slightly higher temperatures. Most flower from autumn to spring.

Top: **Cymbidium** *'Red Beauty' (C): a vigorous, free-flowering variety.*

Left: **Cymbidium** *'Sarah Jean Sprite' (C).*

Cymbidium *Robin 'Freckles' (C): an unusual cymbidium whose flowers display markings rather than an even colour.*
Page opposite: **Cymbidium** *Luis Graves 'Waikanae' (C): strong-growing, upright spikes produced by a medium-sized plant.*
Below: **Cymbidium** *Dignity 'Barbara' (C): a standard-sized* **cymbidium** *whose flowers are distinctively edged with white.*

sphagnum moss, but this is not usually necessary. For those plants that need more moisture in the root zone, the addition of chopped sphagnum moss is useful, although care must be taken since this material can break down in a way that can cause root death. Sometimes sick plants can be resuscitated in loosely packed sphagnum moss; some growers use only this material with success.

Before you use bark, it should be soaked in water to remove toxic tannins, preferably with some high-nitrogen fertiliser. Damp but well-drained mix should be used to repot, since a wet mix creates problems as it will not flow around the roots.

Most bark mixes have an effective life of three to four years, as normal decomposition will gradually break the material down

A **cymbidlum** plant removed from a pot, showing strong, healthy root growth.

to the point that it starts to hold a lot of water and thus excludes air from the roots, which will eventually kill them. Regular renewal of the mix is essential. If you move the plant to a larger container, replace all the mix; do not just add more. Small plants respond to repotting every three to six months with increased growth, this will reduce the time to maturity and flowering by six to twelve months or so.

Most cultivated orchids would grow naturally on trees, so these are often grown on slabs of tree fern fibre, cork bark or even actual tree branches. Some plants prefer this method, which can be an attractive variation to an orchid collection. In most areas tree fern fibre slabs are most suitable, although the slabs must be well weathered , as fresh material can cause damage to roots. Generally, slabs are cut 20 to 30 mm thick, with copper or plastic-coated wire inserted to allow them to be hung. Plants can be attached to a slab by:

- cutting a small flap in the mount and wedging the plant into this; or
- tying the plant on with monofilament fishing line, copper or thin plastic-covered wire, or suitable pieces of nylon stocking.

A small pad of sphagnum moss over and under the roots can provide extra moisture and humidity required for re-establishment. Take care with this material as it can break down quickly, especially if a heavy-fertilising regime is followed. Such pads should be removed as soon as new roots penetrate the mount. Newly mounted plants should be kept in a warm and shady spot and should be misted daily, until new root growth is apparent .

PAPHIOPEDILUMS

These are the popular lady slipper orchids. The single-flowered, green-leaved, cool-growing varieties are best for beginners. The mottled-leave form and multiflowered, green-leave form are intermediate to warm growing.

Top: **Paphiopedilum hirsutissimum** (C): *a species with plain green leaves and strongly coloured flowers, suitable for growers with limited facilities.*
Left: **Paphiopedilum** *'St Swithin'(1): a green-leaved, multiflowering species producing large, attractive flowers.*

Paphiopedilum 'Alma Gaevert'(*1*): an attractive, mottled-leaved 'Maudiae' variety. *Pages overleaf: A **dendrobium** hybrid.*

REPOTTING

Plant repotting is required when:
- it has outgrown the existing container or mount; or
- the existing medium has broken down.

Repotting is a practice feared by many new growers. While many orchid plants look delicate, in reality they are tough and can survive an amazing amount of abuse, although this should be avoided as much as possible. If repotting is a worry, visit an established grower or go to a local orchid exhibition where this procedure is very often demonstrated.

If a plant has grown too large for an existing pot, you can transfer it to a larger container, although there may be practical limitations on the size of plant or container that can be accommodated. Usually, it is best to divide the plant. Break the rhizome between the pseudobulbs after the plant has been removed from the container. Sometimes, if you plan ahead, you can cut the rhizome in late winter or early spring and dust the cut with flowers of sulphur or another similar fungicide, without separating the parts. The cut portion may break into new growth so when the parts are separated they will re-establish much more quickly. If you do cut the plant, remember to flame the knife between plants, to prevent the spread of virus.

Each piece of plant should comprise a new lead (growing point) and three to six old pseudobulbs, since small divisions may not be large enough to flower the following year. Single pseudobulbs will usually grow but will take three to four years to reach flowering size again. Single or small groups of pseudobulbs can often be encouraged to grow if put into a closed plastic bag with some damp sphagnum moss, then placed in a warm shaded area. When new roots reach 25 to 35 mm long, repot normally.

Some orchids, especially some *dendrobiums*, form small plants along the pseudobulbs. Once their roots reach 15 to 20 mm long, these plants can be removed and potted separately. Also, old pseudobulbs can often be removed and placed in damp sphagnum moss in a warm place. After a month or so many will produce new plants.

All repotting should be completed just as new growth commences, usually in the spring. If the mix has broken down at other times of the year, repotting must be done then, but every attempt should be made to ensure the plant has become re-established before the winter. If a base-heater is available, place repotted plants on the heater, this will allow repotting virtually all year, although the period of most active root growth ensures maximum success.

The actual repotting process is relatively simple. Remove the plant from the container—you may have to knock it on a

THE GROWTH PROCESS TYPICAL OF MOST ORCHIDS

PSEUDOBULB WITH NEW GROWTH ON ONE SIDE.

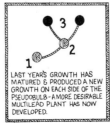

LAST YEAR'S GROWTH HAS MATURED & PRODUCED A NEW GROWTH ON EACH SIDE OF THE PSEUDOBULB - A MORE DESIRABLE MULTILEAD PLANT HAS NOW DEVELOPED.

IN THE FOLLOWING YEAR THE LATEST PSEUDOBULBS HAVE PRODUCED NEW GROWTHS. THREE LEADS HAVE NOW DEVELOPED.

KEY

- - - RHIZOME
PSEUDOBULB
● GROWTH
1 YEAR

bench, then press the sides of the pot to release the attached roots. Gently remove all the mix using either your fingers or a jet of water. All dead roots should be removed. Live roots are white or light brown; dead roots are black, soft and flattened. Try to do as little damage as possible to live roots. If they are very long, you can cut the ends. Cut or damaged roots will usually branch and regrow quickly.

Choose a pot that is large enough for the next two or three years' growth. It may be advantageous to burn extra drainage holes in the container. Clean drainage can be assured by placing some large pieces of bark or similar material in the bottom of the container. Place the plant so that there is sufficient room for forward growth, with the rhizome some 15 mm below the rim; pour in the mix, ensuring it flows around the roots. This can be assisted by knocking the pot on the bench or tapping the sides. Gradually fill up the container until the rhizome is just covered. Place stakes, if required, in the pot before filling as later insertion can damage roots. Do not pack the mix too tightly—as an occasional test, you should be able to pick up a repotted plant by the leaves and only one or two times in ten should it come out of the pot. Place the repotted plant in a warm, shaded area, mist the foliage daily and resume watering when new growth is apparent.

Do not forget to label all divisions as a plant without a name loses much of its value, note also the date of repotting. Try to use the same type of pots and potting mix. Variation makes watering and other cultivation more difficult as each plant will have different requirements.

WATERING

Correct watering is often the most difficult aspect to cover. Each grower's watering habits, growing area and potting mixes have their own distinctive characteristics. Some thought and care will establish what is necessary.

Many commonly cultivated orchids originate from countries where the natural habitats are subject to a summer monsoon, whose seasonal characteristics should be duplicated if possible. These conditions may be different from your climate.

In regions where summers are warm and dry, remember that a summer monsoon produces warm wet conditions.

Winters in monsoon areas are cool and dry, this should be compared with winter conditions in your region.

Between these seasonal extremes there are often drier periods, which you should take into account.

*Two pseudobulbs broken from a **cymbidium**.*

DENDROBIUMS

Australian native *dendrobiums*-cool and intermediate types-are widely grown. There is a wide selection of other *dendrobiums* spanning the full temperature range. Both single and multiflowered spikes are produced by the many varieties.

Top: **Dendrobium speciosum** *(C-1):*
the large-growing .'Rock Lily' orchid, which bears numerous spikes with many flowers.
Left: **Dendrobium kingianum** *(C):*
a species which quickly produces large specimens and is recommended as an ideal beginner's orchid because of its ease of cultivation and free-flowering habit.

Above:
Dendrobium *'Lady Hamilton' (I-W):*
a brightly coloured example of the warmer-
growing phalaenopsis type of hybrid
dendrobium.

Left: **Dendrobium bullenianum** *(I-W):*
this Philippine species bears
dense clusters of flowers.

Page opposite:
Dendrobium thrysiflorum *(C-1)*
this Himalayan species produces
magnihcent but short-lived flowers in
many large, pendulous clusters, likes
warm, moist summers and cool winters.

Right:
Dendrobium Cunninghamii *(C):*
a New Zealand native that needs careful
cultivation, producing many variable
flowers on long, thin pseudobulbs.

Coelogyne cristata (C): *a popular species which produces a mass of beautiful flowers.*

Some orchids have heavy, thick leaves with large pseudobulbs, these are storage devices for water, adapted by the plant to suit quite dry environments. These plants must be allowed to partially dry out in between waterings, to have a wet/dry cycle of five to seven days. Other varieties have thin, soft leaves, requiring more frequent watering. Some, like *paphiopedilums*, do not have any pseudobulbs at all, these therefore must be kept moist—but not wet—at all times. More plants are lost to overwatering — that is, watering too often—than by underwatering. For most orchids, especially those with pseudobulbs, a good rule is:

"if in doubt, do not water".

Under hot, dry conditions, spraying plants and their surroundings will maintain humidity and also cool the plants, which most will appreciate. Sometimes slabs can be difficult to water properly, so dunking them in a bucket of water ensures they are really wet.

LIGHT

All plants require light for photosynthesis, but their tolerances can vary. In most areas some protection from a strong midday sun is required, perhaps, 30 per cent shade. Some, like *phalaenopsis*, need more shade—about 50 per cent in bright locations. Watch your plants, they can often tell you if they are not receiving what they require. Long, limp, dark green and floppy foliage indicates too much shade. Hard, compact growths, and yellow leaves, possibly with red pigmentation, indicate too much sun. Unsightly burning of the foliage can occur under these latter circumstances unless high humidity and good air movement are maintained. For most plants, leaves should be a medium yellow-green. With mottled-leaved *paphiopedilums*, strong light reduces the contrast between the leaf zones, while shaded conditions enhance it (although too much shade may reduce flowering). Generally, for most plants, conditions that are brighter than they receive naturally will produce the most flowers.

Flower colour can alter by variations in light levels. In *cymbidiums*, for example, stronger-coloured red, brown, dark pink and bright yellow varieties require bright light during bud development.

White, green and pastel coloured flowers should be shaded during bud development to produce the best results.

During spike elongation, do not alter the orientation of plants. To do so may cause the spikes to assume unattractive shapes, so that flower placement and presentation may become unsatisfactory. Flower spikes often require staking during development, but always allow natural form to develop—some are upright, others gracefully arching or some may be sharply pendulous—since this produces the most attractive display.

FERTILISER

Most orchids respond to fertiliser application, and for most growers "a little often" is the best rule of thumb.

Use a general-purpose garden fertiliser at about half to a third of general strength recommendations. Every month or so flush pots with plenty of fresh water to ensure there is no build-up of undesirable salt concentrations. Both solid and liquid fertilisers can be used; a base dressing of solid fertiliser in the spring and autumn supplemented by foliar dressings are appropriate. Bark mixes require high-nitrogen fertiliser, although the nitrogen should be reduced during bud initiation (for example, in summer for *cymbidiums*) and the potash content increased.

PESTS AND DISEASES

Most orchids are subject to relatively few pests and diseases. Some, like *cymbidiums*, can become infested by the two-spotted spider mite and red spider mite.

The effects of these on *cymbidiums* can be reduced if humidity is increased around the growing areas by misting the plants, especially undersides of the foliage and the plant's surroundings. If these pests become established, use of chemical control will be necessary. See your local garden centre for an appropriate product; two applications seven to ten days apart will usually suffice.

Most garden chemicals are satisfactory, however, always test new products on a few representative plants before application.

Scale and mealy bug infestations may occur occasionally. Again, use of chemicals to control these attacks may be necessary.

Some bacterial rots and fungi can infect collections, especially if environmental conditions or general hygiene is less than ideal. If you are experiencing difficulties, first check your environment, then your growing facilities before using a lot of chemicals. It may be that simple measures such as slightly warmer conditions, greater air movement, or a change in watering regime (earlier in the day to ensure that plants are dry before nightfall), rather than expensive chemicals, is required.

Virus is a serious disease which cannot be treated. Primarily it is spread by the dissemination of infected sap, especially the use of infected cutting tools. All tools should be flamed between plants, and any infected plants should be incinerated, not just thrown on the compost heap. You can have a plant tested for virus if you believe it may have infected your collection.

When you obtain new plants, check for any disease, if necessary keeping them in a separate quarantine area for a month or so to ensure they are pathogen-free .

If you have to resort to chemicals, ensure that you observe all safety precautions. It is the bugs you want to kill, not you, your family or friends.

Page opposite: **Cattleya loddigesii** *(1): a typical bifoliate type which appreciates warmth and plenty of water during spring and summer, but which tolerates cool conditions during winter when it is dormant.*

CATTLEYA ALLIANCE

This large alliance includes **cattleyas**, **laelias**, **sophronitis** and **brassavolas**, among others, all of which interbreed. They range from spectacular, large, single-flowered specimens to multiflowered varieties.

Top: **Laelia kautskyi** *(1):*
a brightly coloured species laelia which grows naturally on exposed rock surfaces.

Left: **Leptotes bicolor** *(1):*
an attractive, small-growing, terete leaved orchid which thrives on tree fern mounts.

Above: **Cattleya 'Colworth'** *(1):*
a strong-growing hybrid **cattleya** *of the single-leaved type.*
Below: S1c *(***Naomi Kerns 'Fireball'*** x **Laelia albida***) (1):*
a strongly coloured variety taking the **laelia** *shape.*

Above: S1 'My Little Pumpkin' (1)
a brightly coloured cluster variety which stands out in any company.
*Below: **Sophronitis coccinea** (C):*
a brightly coloured Brazilian species which grows naturally on high mountains and likes cool,
humid conditions with plenty of air movement.

S1 Jinn (C-1): a colourful hybrid typically producing masses of eye-catching flowers.

S1c Jewel Box 'Scheherazade' (1):
a popular, brightly coloured hybrid
*produced by crossing a **sophronitis** with*
*a **cattleya** and a **laelia**.*

PLANT PROPAGATION

Orchid seeds are minute. They contain no plant food, as they rely on specific fungi to break down food to forms the seed can use. You cannot sow orchid seeds as you would for most plants in a garden. Most orchid seed is planted by specially equipped laboratories into sterile flasks to germinate. You can do this yourself, but it requires special knowledge and facilities, usually beyond the reach of most growers. These laboratories are able to take seed to a stage where the seedlings can be easily taken out and grown to maturity.

Contents of orchid flasks vary between one or two plants, or as many as fifty or sixty. Obviously small flasks will suit most amateur growers. Sterile flasks must remain sealed until plant growth reaches the top of the container, when they are ready to plant out—this can take between six to twelve months from initial sowing.

Individual plants from a flask of seedlings of a single cross will show variation in final flower colour and shape. It is this variety that makes the purchase of a flask and the challenge of growing seedlings to flowering size an exciting experience. With such a variety there may be only one outstanding plant from a single cross .

A separate laboratory process is used that allows identical copies of a single selected individual plant to be propagated. These 'mericlones' can be purchased in a flask.

Because they are selected plants, usually each plant will be more expensive, but each mericlone of the same plant will be not similar, but identical.

If you purchase a flask of seedlings or mericlones, keep it in a warm, sheltered location. Once the plants fill the flask, they must be removed. Both seedlings and mericlones are deflasked the same way.

Removing plants must be completed with care to ensure maximum survival. Several days before removal, the flask should be opened. It will act as a glasshouse as the process of plant establishment to their more exposed environment begins.

Before removing plants from the flask, there is some basic task preparation.

You will need:

1. A hammer or vice to break narrow necked flasks. Wide-necked containers allow the removal of plants without destruction of the flasks.
2. Some paper to protect yourself as the flask is broken, also paper on which to place the extracted plants.
3. A bowl of water containing fungicide. While plants are sterile on removal, they may be damaged during deflasking, allowing pathogens in; a fungicide dip

*Page opposite: **Laelia anceps** (C-1)*
a popular and widely grown Mexican species which likes plenty of sun.

prevents problems developing.

4. Suitable growing media. Bark mixes, suitably sterilised (in an oven or pressure cooker) then moistened, are satisfactory. Use a mix slightly finer than you would use for mature plants.

5. Suitable growing containers. Thumb pots should be used for individual plants; 75 to 100 mm squat pots for group planting.

Break the flask, or from a wide-necked container, remove the plants. Wash all attached agar from the roots, then dip the plants in fungicide and allow them to dry on the paper.

You may either:

- place the whole unsorted clump in a squat pot, as undisturbed plants growing together may establish more quickly; or
- separate plants, grade by size, then place them in a 75 to 100 mm "community pot"; or
- separate plants then place them in individual small containers.

Remember to label all plants.

Place pots of plants in a plastic tent, but open the bag for a little longer each day as the plants are re-established. Such a tent ensures provision of the higher humidity that they require. If all goes well, new roots will develop rapidly. As this happens, the plants should be provided with normal growing conditions. Most plants appreciate bottom heat if it is available; this reduces the time needed to reach flowering size by some months. Once new roots are formed, normal watering can be commenced rather than the initial misting provided, and dilute fertiliser can be applied. Most plants will appreciate repotting in new media every three to six months. This ensures the fastest growth rate. Seedlings or mericlones

will reach flowering size in three to six years.

It is a unique attraction of orchids that their parentage, and that of all hybrids can be registered in a 'stud book',
Sander's Lists of Orchid Hybrids.
Any man-made hybrid can be researched or ancestry traced, back to its component species. Such studies can be fascinating, and are essential if a serious breeding programme is being attempted.

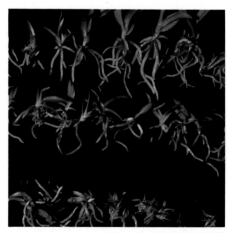

*These **cattleya** seedlings
have been removed from a flask.
Note the significant variation in plant size.*

PHALAENOPSIS

The so-called moth orchids are distinctive,
quick-growing plants with attractive flowers. They require warm temperatures.

Phalaenopsis (Dorset Bride x Zwingle) x (Aglow x Dragon Tongue) (W):
a colourful, warm-growing hybrid with large flowers.

SOURCES OF PLANTS AND INFORMATION

Many orchids are commercially available from garden centres or specialist orchid nurseries. Societies have been established where orchid growers are able to develop their interest. Orchid plants are offered for sale at their meetings and exhibitions.

There are advantages to purchasing plants there as you are able to see what can be grown successfully in your locality, with first-hand specialist advice available from the grower. There is also a wide range of published orchid literature, which will provide additional information on this fascinating family of plants. These publications offer specific advice for the particular plants you choose to grow.

Enjoy orchids; they are not hard to grow, neither are they expensive, nor do they require extensive growing facilities. Their magnificent flowers are sure to provide hours of enjoyment for you, your family and friends.

*Above: **Maxillaria picta** (1):*
a distinctively coloured species which produces a most delightful fragrance.
*Page opposite: **Phaius tankervilleae** (1):*
a large Australian terrestrial species producing tall, attractive flower spikes.

ONCIDIUMS

This is a variable group, including many attractive plants with spectacular, long-lasting flowers. They range from cool- to warm-growing types.

Top: **Oncidium rhinocerotes** *(C):*
a cluster of typical yellow flowers each bearing an upthrust 'rhinoceros horn'.

Right: **Oncidium pubes** *(1):*
a pendulous, compact, autumn flowering species which appreciates a long root run when mounted on a tree fern slab.

Oncidium (*spilopterum* x *crispum*) (*C-1*):
a brightly coloured primary hybrid showing the typical
oncidium *yellow lip but with contrasting colours.*

LYCASTES

This group is becoming increasingly popular. There are both cool and intermediate types with many bright, eye-catching flowers.

Top: **Anguloa clowesii** *(1):*
a species closely related to **Iycaste***, producing bright yellow, tuliplike flowers, each with a fascinating mobile lip.*
Left: **Lycaste** *'Concentration' (1): a large-flowered hybrid* **Lycaste** *whose pseudobulbs become larger each year when it is correctly cultivated.*

INDEX

The page numbers in **bold** type indicate illustrations.

Aërides 'Amy Ede'   **11**
Anguloa clowesii (1)   **46**
Aranda (Arachnis x Vanda)   **15**
aranda hybrid   **7**
bacteria rot   33
brassavolas   34
bud development   31
CATTLEYA ALLIANCE   34
Cattleyas   9, 34
   'Colworth' (1)   **35**
   loddigesii (1)   **33**
   seedlings   **40**
chemical control   33
Coelogyne cristata (C)   **30**
CYMBIDIUMS   17
Cymbidium   9,13, 16, **20**, 31, 33
   Dignity 'Barbara'   **18**
   Luis Graves 'Waikanae'   **18**
   'Red Beauty'   **17**
   Robin 'Freckles'   **18**
   'Sarah Jean Sprite'   **17**
   Touchstone 'Mahogany'   **9**

DENDROBIUMS   27
Dendrobium   **4**, 23
   'arachnites'   **12**
   bullenianum (I-W)   **29**
   Cunninghamii (C)   **29**
   'Ellen'   **10**
   hybrid   **22**
   kingianum (C)   **27**
   'Lady Hamilton' (I-W)   **29**
   speciosum (C-1)   **27**
   thrysiflorum (C-1)   **29**
epiphytes   12
exhibitions   43
Fertiliser   31
fungi   33
general hygiene   33
Growing Facilities   15
   Media   16
laboratories   39
Laelia   34, **35**
   anceps (C-1)   **39**
   kautskyi (1)   **34**

Leptotes bicolor (1)   **34**
Light   30
LYCASTES   46
Lycaste   **46**
   'Concentration' (1)   **46**
Maudiae   **22**
Maxillaria picta (1)   **43**
mealy bug   33
mericlones   39, 40
MONOPODIAL   9
moth orchid   **41**
Naomi Kerns 'Fireball' x Laelia albida   **35**
ONCIDIUMS   44
Oncidium (spilopterum x crispum) (C-1)   **45**
   pubes (1)   **44**
   rhinocerotes (C)   **44**
   stramineum x aurisasinorum   **13**
orchid literature   43
orchid nurseries   43
Orchid seeds   39
orientation   31
PAPHIOPEDILUMS   21
Paphiopedilum   13, 30, 31
   'Alma Gaevert'(1)   **22**
   'concolor'   **12**
   hirsutissimum (C)   **21**
   'St Swithin'(1)   **21**

Phaius tankervilleae (1)   **43**
PHALAENOPSIS   41
phalaenopsis   9, 13, 30
   (Dorset Bride x Zwingle) x
   (Aglow x Dragon Tongue)(W)   **41**
pigmentation   31
Pleione formosana   10
Pseudobulbs   11, 23, **26**
Pterostylis graminea   **9**
Red spider mite   33
Repotting   23
rhizome   26
S1 Jinn (C-1)   **37**
S1 'My Little Pumpkin' (1)   **36**
S1c Jewel Box 'Scheherazade' (1)   **37**
Sander's Lists of Orchid Hybrids   40
Sarcochilus ceciliae   **13**
   hartmanii   **7**
Scale   33
Sophronitis   34
   coccinea (C)   **36**
spider mite   33
SYMPODIAL   9
Temperatures   15
vanda   **4**, 9
Virus   33
Watering   26